The Power of Visual Presentation

TONY HORTON • PORTFOLIO

The Power of Visual Presentation

TONY HORTON • PORTFOLIO

Visual Reference Publications, Inc., New York

Copyright © 2001 by Visual Reference Publications, Inc.

Visual Reference Publications, Inc.
302 Fifth Avenue
New York, NY 10001

Distributors to the trade in the United States and Canada
Watson-Guptill
770 Broadway
New York, NY 10003

Distributors outside the United States and Canada
HarperCollins International
10 East 53 Street
New York, NY 10022-5299

Book Design: Harish Patel Design Associates, New York

Library of Congress Cataloging in Publication Data:
The Power of Visual Presentation
Printed in China
ISBN 1-58471-007-1

Introduction 6
T L Horton Design, Inc. Offices 8
Preface 12

Retail Store Design 13
B C Sports Collectables 14
ZAP 20
Java City 24
Successories 26

Environmental Graphic Design 33
Union Station 34
York Galleria 42
The Pavilion 50
Southland Mall 54
Southgate 60
West End Marketplace 62
Regency Square 68

Exhibit Design 73
Landau Heyman 74
Melvin Simon & Associates 76
LaSalle Partners 80
MEPC 82
Pyramid 86
Westfield 90
Trammell Crow 94
L J Hooker 98
Heitman Properties 102
Homart 106
Herring Marathon 110
Equity Properties 114
Enterprise 118
Glimcher 120
Rockwell Collins 126
Equity Properties 134

Kiosk Design 139
Disney, Beauty & the Beast 140
Equity Properties 144
York Town Mall 146
Montgomery Mall 148
Annapolis Mall 150
Cleveland Indians 152
Fairfield Commons 154
Tyson Galleria 156
Copley Place 160
Great Mall of The Great Plains 162
Fremont Street Experience 164
Sierra Vista Mall 167
Successories, Garden State Mall 168
Westside Pavilion 170

Awards 172
Selected Bibliography, Publications 173
Selected Bibliography, Books 174
Selected project List 176
Acknowledgements 178
Photography Credits 179
Index by Projects 180

Introduction

*I*f Tony Horton had been a baseball star instead of a designer, he would have earned his own special niche in the Hall of Fame: Tony would have been a hybrid – a combination of the reliable and consistent players with the superstars who could "step – up" and do whatever it took to win a game.

As a 25 - year shopping center and real estate professional, I have never known anyone who was such a consistent and reliable all-star in so many design areas as Tony Horton. Whether Tony was creating a new trade show – corporate identity design, a retail kiosk design program, or any aspect of the design program for a shopping center redevelopment/renovation, the results were always certain …The final program would surely be creative, innovative, tasteful, and "dead – on target" as the right solution.

In thinking about Tony Horton in relation to this introduction, I always returned to one of the issues of Tony's essence: "What was it about him that made him so wonderful at so many architectural, design, and related design areas?" The fundamental truth is that Tony Horton is an extraordinary and gifted artist. More often than not, Tony found solutions to visual challenges that were elegant and practical, at the same time.

I have known Tony Horton for over 15 years, having been introduced by a mutual friend and shopping center industry marketing icon, Cheri Morris. I was working in Chicago investor Sam Zell's organization at that time. I was tasked with helping to build a great operating company to capitalize upon the retail assets that Zell was acquiring. As I began to focus on company identity, Tony was introduced to me as THE "corporate – identity/trade show guru." After one meeting, I was fairly convinced that Tony was a trade show wizard. When I got the drawings, I knew that it was so.

*I*n the years that followed, I had the privilege of working with Tony on further – ranging projects that included the first retail kiosks, or RMUs [Retail Merchandising Units], and several shopping center redevelopment/renovations. Tony Horton always exhibited his own special version of the type of competent and experienced design acumen that clients always seek from top architectural and graphics firms in the re-creation of properties and projects. It is worth noting that regardless of the nature of the deadline or scope of the challenge, Tony always exhibited two further noteworthy traits: Tony Horton truly listened to his client's perspective and he was always unflappable, in any situation.

From a very personal perspective, working with Tony Horton, and Sharon Polonia, an associate in Zell's company, on the very first "RMU," retail merchandising unit, represents the highlight of my career in the shopping center business. We had figured out, before involving Tony, that the shopping center industry needed a replacement for the ancient, wheeled pushcarts that were dominant since the Middle Ages. Tony proved himself to possess both "design vision" and the "soul of a merchant" in relation to the RMU project and many others, thereafter.

Tony always exhibited an advanced degree in what I will call *Retail Ergonomics,* or an ability to produce twin solutions that maximized visual impact upon consumers, while providing practical working solutions for merchants.

*O*ften, when we chatted during those days, Tony would profess the desire to escape the limitations of the Trade Show business and to replace them with the more artistic large-scale renovation program projects. The whole scenario still causes me to smile because I always viewed Tony's capabilities as extraordinary in being able to create dazzling 3D advertising and identity art within the constraints of "booth sculpture" and budgets. Just as Sir Arthur Conan Doyle's public never allowed him to retire Sherlock Holmes when he wanted to move on, I always assumed that Tony's resounding and well known success in the Trade Show sector would never support an easy exit.

Over the history of the Shopping Center business, I know of no other designer who has had such dramatic impact upon the course of so many important areas of its evolution. Today, environmental graphics are a fundamental point of differentiation in the creation of most new or renovation shopping center projects. Tony Horton's first RMU has evolved into and created the dominant temporary kiosk format in the entire shopping center industry.

I have always viewed Tony as an artist, first. It certainly appears that, at last, Tony has the ability to focus all of his energy upon his artistic pursuits.

I am looking forward to the next phase of Tony's artistry.

Mark N. London

T L Horton Design, Inc.
Offices
Dallas, TX

*W*orking within an open warehouse space, designer Tony Horton created this unique setting for his firm's offices and design studio. "Creating an environment that encourages creative minds and functions as a business can be very difficult. It is as important to provide visual stimuli to your employees as it is to impress your clients."

Since the firm would design and fabricate, the offices had to be located in an industrial warehouse district. The challenge was "to fabricate a free standing structure within the warehouse, providing areas for studios, offices, galleries and administrative spaces." The entire space was built in modules allowing for flexibility and expansion.

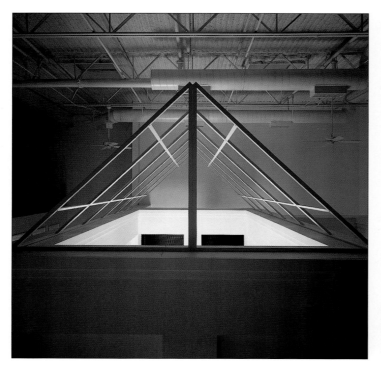

Semi-translucent dividers provide privacy for the lower offices without decreasing light levels.

"Our environment was mostly open, creating interaction on both levels. Learning to work together is important and an open environment encourages verbal and visual interaction." Open stairways connect the levels and offices between floors. Skylights mounted in the warehouse ceiling illuminate the space with white light helping designers in selection of colors and materials. The gallery on the lower level is "capped" with a metal pediment fabricated from steel angle. The open framework allows light to penetrate the gallery space.

The interior space was painted a pure white, allowing any addition of color to stand out.

PREFACE

*I*n approaching any design project, my objective is to create designs that bring success to my clients. In creating designs that work, I always consider how the design will impact its market. What materials and colors appeal to the audience? How does the architecture relate to the viewer? How does the architecture relate to its surroundings? Will it turn people away, or will it attract them? Will it complement the environment or will it visually stand out? With the knowledge of how the design effects its market and its surroundings, you can create a design that is truly successful.

For the past twenty-three years I have been very fortunate to work on a wide variety of projects. Focusing my design career primarily on work for the Shopping Center, Retail and Trade Show industries, I have designed everything from simple push carts to complete shopping center environments. My work has always focused on combining graphics, color, architecture and lighting.

Each audience responds differently to the use of colors and materials. It is important to understand the likes and dislikes of your market in creating any design that will work to its maximum potential. You can easily effect the motions and reactions of people with the use of lighting and materials. Although it is impossible to totally control the actions of your target audience, you can predict with fair success how they will react to certain visual stimuli.

We are all influenced subconsciously by our senses. Each of us, based on our backgrounds, are influenced by different colors, lighting and shapes. If we can see it, touch it or smell it, it can effect our judgement and our decision making. The power of visual presentation is a powerful tool, key to successful design.

Tony Horton

RETAIL STORE DESIGN

"Successful retail store design combines the usage of architecture, fixtures, color and graphics with the retailer's image and product mix.

The objective for the designer is to create sales by designing an environment that encourages shoppers to develop a personal relationship with the store.

Understanding the client, and the client's market is fundamental in creating an atmosphere that will be successful. Different markets respond differently to visual stimuli. It is important to modify your designs to fit the likes and dislikes of the specific market."

B C Sports Collectables
Bear, PA

*W*ith the public's greatest interest in sports, sports memorabilia and collectibles, the B C Sports Collectables store designed by Tony Horton combines sports and collectibles in a smart exciting retail environment. History is teamed with whimsy in this contemporary interior, where primary colors accentuate the black and white palette warmed by the maple laminate finishes.

Valuable collectible cards are protected and displayed in vertical cases located adjacent to each sport category.

The cash station is prominently marked by yellow "Goal Posts" that support the store's identification signage.

The crisp white 5000 sq. ft. interior showcases vintage black and white photo murals, historical collector's items, sports uniforms and comics. Every element was designed for the presentation of merchandise and also to integrate with the overall sports theme. All the major sports are represented and color coded to allow shoppers quick visual access to their sports interest.

The collectible uniforms are shown in mock sports lockers providing display areas for specific "soft" merchandise.

The low ceiling was left exposed to provide maximum ceiling visibility. The mechanical and support trusses are left exposed and painted black. The walls are erected all the way to the deck, giving the viewer the sense of increased height in the store.

Concealed neon accentuates the upper level walls, allowing some visibility to the support structures.

Sports action and history are emphasized with the larger than life size black and white photo murals along two sides of the store, creating 20 ft. of graphics that celebrate great moments in sports. Collectible cards are displayed in vertical display cases illuminated by halogen lamps. The relationship between the peripheral wall height and the building's trusses and light fixtures suspended in the space, create a theatrical stage for exhibiting product displays.

Products are divided by size in different merchandising displays. Tall displays were designed to display cards, and low displays were designed to display boxed products. All cases are defined with an identification ribbon, utilizing different colors for each sport.

Large sports murals help direct traffic through the store.

Vertical cases displaying sports cards divide each sport section, creating a defined path between each section.

ZAP

STRATOSPHERE HOTEL/CASINO
LAS VEGAS, NV

*L*ocated in the Stratosphere Shopping Center in Las Vegas, NV, Zap produces and sells custom embroidered caps.

An overscaled entry feature was designed to give punch to this small specialty store. Designed to complement the shopping center's art deco corridor, columns are clad with rings of brushed aluminum. Twelve ft. doors open directly to each of the three performance stations. "Create your own cap" identifies each of the stations.

Multiple logos are used on the interior and exterior to build product and company name recognition. Four display cases located in front of the store display examples of caps that can be produced.

Hard rock maple laminate, with black and white, create an environment promoting a strong presentation of the cap graphics.

The signage "Create Your Own Cap," quickly identifies the store's function. The interior signage helps to move shoppers through the limited space, from the ordering of the cap to the production and ultimate payment and pick-up.

The lighting was designed to spotlight products and enhance the theatrical quality in this interactive, high-tech environment.

The store is exaggerated due to the 16 ft. ceilings and 12 ft. wall fixtures. This usage of space presents a strong image to product and identification. Rows of embroidered caps line two walls, displaying a large inventory. Caps located in display cases next to each performance station are open in front to give customers the ability to handle different caps.

Monitors mounted to stainless steel columns show the graphic design process, and allow the customer to participate in the design.

JAVA CITY
PHILADELPHIA, PA

*C*reated for the Aramark Corporation, this coffee concept store was designed to complement the store's logo. The condiment counter, located adjacent to the service counter reflects the shape of the logo, helping build name recognition. The angled shape of the service counters further accentuates the logo design.

An angled light fixture located at the end of the service counter encourages customers to enter the store, and helps identify the location of the condiment counter.

The store fixtures are finished with maple laminate, stainless steel and black accents. The counter tops are fabricated from cast plastic. Hard stock maple arms support the counter and help define the design direction.

An angled wall, finished in the same neutral color as the perimeter walls, conceals a workstation. A menu board finished with a black matte laminate contrasts with the menu listing, produced from white vinyl. Each portion of the interior work stations are designed for specific functions, making the best use of the limited space.

SUCCESSORIES
PRUDENTIAL CENTER
BOSTON, MA

*S*uccessories designs, produces and retails motivational materials, tapes, books, executive organizers, plaques, posters, postcards and apparel. All products are targeted for creating success. The design objective for Tony Horton was to create a store image with the atmosphere of success in a state-of-the-art shopping environment.

The dramatic symmetry between the entrance and the interior fixtures provides a unified presentation. The custom light fixtures that flank the entrance to the store provide immediate visibility to the storefront identification. The angled glass window panels add a unique scale to the storefront and provide a strong presentation to the window displays.

For the store's palette, Horton specified a deep stained hard stock cherry wood with accents of black and copper with a verdi patina finish. A warm zolatone paint finish is used on the columns to add value and durability. The plastic laminate used on the slat wall fixtures resembles copper with a verdi patina.

This prototype store was planned to work effectively in spaces from 1000 sq. ft. to 1800 sq. ft. All display components and fixtures were designed to be interchangeable. The entire store was designed to be completely fabricated in a shop, including the front entrance. Once the basic on-site work (sheetrock, mechanical and flooring) was completed, all display components and fixturing was installed in less than a week. Producing stores in this manner can reduce the overall cost per square foot, decrease the production time, and allow for less internal management.

Custom light boxes display information about posters located in the rack below. Back illuminated graphics add strength to the information, attracting customers to the display.

Halogen lights are used to add depth and dimension as well as highlights and shadows. To soften the overall ambient light, custom fixtures were created for the store. The lamp shade was fabricated from translucent plexiglass and the base is finished with a powder coated copper patina.

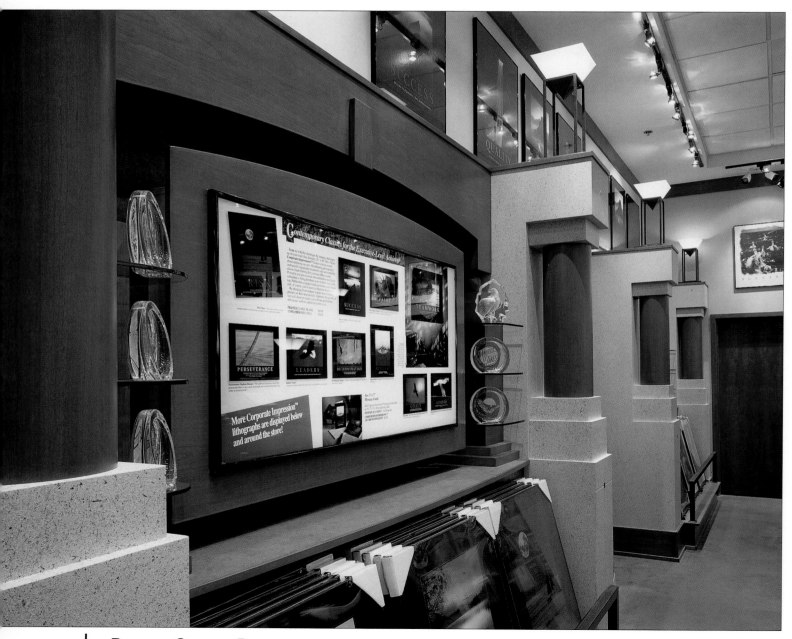

Successories' message is "Our goal is to help you reach yours," and Horton reinforces this message with a store design that projects a first class image in an effective retail environment. The realistic materials along with expert lighting create an atmosphere for both customer and client.

ENVIRONMENTAL GRAPHIC DESIGN

"Environmental graphic design is the combination of sculpture, signage, graphics, lighting, furniture and color working together to complement the architecture.

Good environmental graphic design should produce an environment that provides a pleasurable experience for the shopper, encouraging longer visits and increased sales.

It is important to create an environment that is visually stimulating, providing the components necessary to inform and direct shoppers through the shopping center."

UNION STATION
INDIANAPOLIS, IN

The primary design focus for Horton was to transform the 220,000 sq. ft. Union Station into an exciting, vital and functioning retail center. The Union Station is a landmark structure that is over 100 years old and part of one of the nation's oldest railway systems. The historical aspects of the center had to be maintained and all facade and color treatment within the center had to be approved by the local and state historical societies.

New storefronts, graphics and directional signage were created to revitalize the environment and create an overall identity. Individual identities were designed for each of the merchants in the retail areas and vendors in the 70,000 sq. ft. food court. The objective was to create an atmosphere that enticed shoppers to stay for extended periods of time, to shop, eat and be entertained.

To simplify the maze of mechanical and structural elements, color was used to define and separate the features. Coordinated colors and graphics were added to create a fun and exciting environment.

Since the structure was landmark protected and could not be physically altered, none of the new elements could be attached directly to the existing building or its structural parts. All new signage and architectural elements had to be pressure fitted.

The existing entrance to the train boarding stations was enhanced by a new Union Station logo. This stairwell connects the second level food court with the main retail level. The logo combines bright, fresh colors with neon and theatrical lamps. The sculptural "ghost" from a previous renovation of the station commemorates a bye-gone era of train travel.

To improve the light level, all ceiling mechanical and structural elements were painted in 11 different colors.

The train docks and the passenger loading areas were converted into a food court. A graphic version of a 40 ft. dining car with 20 booths provides additional seating in the food court. Platforms on the ends of the train cars provide space for entertainment venues.

Throughout, color, graphics and signage are used to clarify and delineate retail spaces and to provide easily understandable way-finding information. A total of 33 colors are used to create this exciting retail environment.

Painting the overhead mechanical structure helps visually increase the height level in the retail corridors creating increased traffic flow.

In order to gain additional retail space without adding to the actual space available, custom retail kiosks were added around existing columns. Directories were added in corridors to provide information. A new color palette was chosen to refresh the existing architecture and coordinate with the graphic package.

The graphic program was created by Tony Horton to promote the history of the center and to provide a festive quality to the space. New awnings, banners, ceiling decor, directional signage, and graphics work together to establish a retail environment, and add a revitalized look to the Union Station.

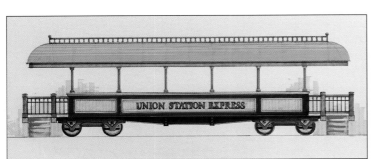

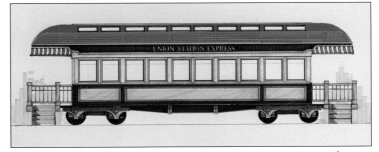

YORK GALLERIA
YORK, PA

*T*he York Galleria needed an environmental graphic program to complete the renovation of this galleria-style shopping center. Neutral in color with a white ceiling and a continuous vaulted skylight, the center was beautiful but lacked sufficient visual stimuli to interest shoppers or to promote traffic flow. There was no sense of direction or source of ready information. Graphics, informational signage and decorative accents were necessary to make the space function properly.

Using graphics influenced by the good luck star symbols painted on local barns, Horton created graphics in two-and three-dimensional formats that relate to the surrounding area.

A 16 ft. wide medallion suspended over the center court provides the foundation for the graphic program. This graphic is visually divided into quarters and mounted on ceiling trusses under the skylights. This graphic gives dimension to the ceiling and increases traffic flow down the corridors.

The graphics are created from "gator" foam that is cut with a laser and painted with a fire resistant material. Halogen spotlights are added to illuminate each of the graphic sculptures.

Banners are hung along vertical support columns throughout the center. The banners were designed to be changed for seasonal and promotional use.

The colors that are used in the floating starburst graphics are combined again in the custom up-lights that were designed to accentuate the supporting columns. Zolatone painted, these fixtures complement the building and graphics color program.

The illumination from the new light sconces serves to help define the corridors and provide light and shadow that enhance the architecture.

Creating visual breaks throughout the main level of the mall are giant graphic circles decorated with variations on the star theme. Executed in multicolored terrazzo with brass divider strips, these oases for planters and benches are much sought after stops in the traffic flow and activity. Serving as rest stops, they also break up the long visual stretch of mall flooring into interesting segments, encouraging traffic flow through the center.

Bold new food graphics were designed for the food court to attract shoppers. Multi-dimensional food items mounted on checkered background panels unify the graphics. The color palette includes bright colors combined with black and white.

The ribbon identification graphic is 20 ft. wide and contains three-dimensional elements, creating stronger visual impact.

Additional sculptural food graphics are mounted around the column located at the center of the food court, creating an anchor point for the food court graphic program. Checkered light sconces were added to the perimeter columns to complete the design concept.

The Pavilion
Washington, DC

The Pavilion is a multi-level shopping center connected to the Old Post Office, an historic, century-old building located on Pennsylvania Avenue. The large skylight and white interior space creates the perfect environment for colorful graphics and sculpture.

Taking the design theme from the history and pageantry associated with the address, stars and stripes dominate, and the many variations on that theme are presented in a smart contemporary style. The graphics and color were added "to create a sense of patriotic excitement while promoting movement between the multi-levels."

Quarter round caps combined with dimensional stars and stripes serve to anchor the decorative red, blue and pink banners that extend down through the three levels of the center.

Floating below a truss that extends across the escalator is a giant clock garlanded with white stars and red and white stripes mounted on a disk and illuminated with blue neon. This 16 ft. wide sculpture identifies the upper level food court.

In the food court, decorative light sconces were added to the support columns. They feature half round frosted glass panels with smaller red half circles in front. White and yellow sunbursts complete the design motif while the lamp washes the face of the columns with a patterned light created by perforated metal.

The illumination from the skylights adds to the overall effectiveness of the decorative color palette and produces interesting patterns of light and shade. The color palette, limited mainly to red, white, blue, golden yellow and deep pink, stimulates the environment and unifies the many dimensional graphics, sculpture and informational signs.

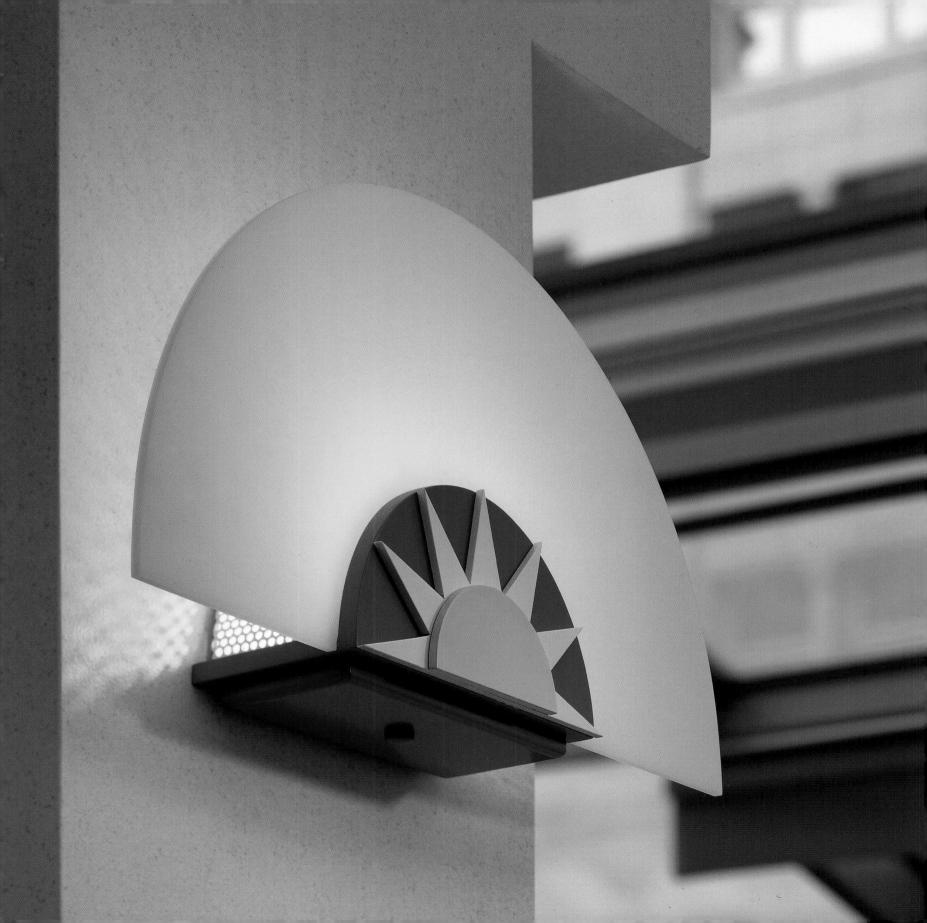

SOUTHLAND MALL
HAYWARD, CA

*T*he food court at Southland Mall was almost invisible, located on a lower level and recessed from view. Visibility was key to creating success for the faltering food court. "The Food Fair" was chosen as the logo since many mall activities would take place in the food court.

To identify the food court location to all corridors, a large three-dimensional food mobile was created and suspended 60 ft. over the center of the court. A 150 ft. long ribbon fabricated from sheet metal was mounted on the upper soffitt and arched entries were added to locate the escalators.

Ten foot tall dimensional food sculptures suspend on aircraft cables 60 ft. over the center of the food court providing grand visibility to the location. The stylized fries, burger, hot dog, ice cream cone, fork and spoon were sculpted from foam and finished in bright colors.

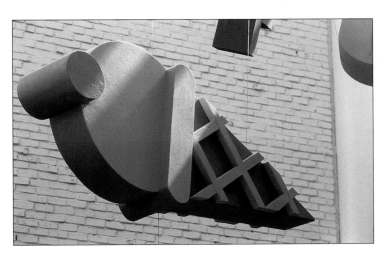

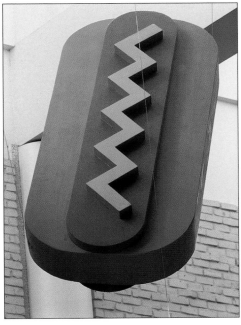

To promote the food vendors and attract shoppers, directories were placed outside the food court on the upper level. The directories are finished in colors that match the graphics of the food court. Back lighted transparencies of the food offerings add incentive for shoppers to visit the food court.

The food court was transformed with color, sculpture and signage into a vital and fun place to visit.

*L*ocated in Sarasota, FL, the winter home of the Ringling Brothers and Barnum & Bailey Circus, is Southgate Mall, renovated from an existing open air strip center. The center was enclosed with light reflective fabric that provides the perfect illumination for highlighting graphic sculpture.

Since the center was once an open air center, retail stores are located on only one side of the center. The walk from one end of the center to the other was long and it was difficult to persuade shoppers to commute the entire distance.

To solve the problem, eight ft. tall tropical birds, fabricated from fiberglass and painted in realistic colors, were suspended throughout the entire corridor, turning the corridor into a large apiary.

Dimensional signage was used to identify the food court. The graphic colors were chosen from the palette used to paint the birds.

WEST END MARKETPLACE
DALLAS, TX

*T*he West End Marketplace is a multi-level shopping center featuring an unusual blend of local and national tenants.

To create an atmosphere with a fun western influence, western icons were designed for use throughout the center in graphics, light fixtures and identification signage. Light coves were created with bent copper sheet metal with an oxidized verdi patina. Western icons were laser cut through the copper and back faced with milk plexiglass. The cove was rear illuminated with white neon. This same treatment appears in the copper bands located between each floor.

In keeping with the building patina, light sconces were fabricated from steel sheet metal and oxidized to produce a rusted finish. Five ft. wide wagon wheel light fixtures were designed with a wagon train scene, laser cut from sheet metal and powder coated. The wagon train was pegged away from the background and rear illuminated with a concealed neon tube, rendering a sunset scene. Light fixtures suspended from the wagon wheel increased light levels above the seating area.

A curved wall was constructed to separate seating areas in the food court. Western icons were sand etched into the glass mounted above the curved wall, and the base was finished with hand-cut ceramic tiles. The wall was necessary to reduce the visual volume of the space and help create intimate dining areas.

Wagon wheel light fixtures were suspended in the main entrance of the center. Recessed halogen lighting was used to illuminate portions of the upper walls providing light and shadow. The neon halo behind the wagon train is easily seen due to the controlled light levels. The circular clock located in the main entrance was constructed from copper sheet metal with laser cut icons. The metal is oxidized to a verdi patina. The halo is created by a neon tube.

Additional column and beam structures were added in the entrance coordinating with the building structure.

REGENCY SQUARE
FLORENCE, AL

*R*egency Square is an enclosed shopping center located in a small southern town. In need of a visual renovation within a limited budget, the design focus was directed on elements that would create change without major demolition. To accomplish this objective, the focus was on the front entrance, flooring and graphics.

Instead of redeveloping the existing architecture of the mall entrances, multi-dimensional signage created the lacking visual strength. The unique design and lighting treatments made a major impact without costly redesign.

A ribbon graphic was used to identify this retail center. The square behind the ribbon was constructed from sheet metal and finished with a painted pattern. Neon and incandescent lighting with strong color makes the signage stand out in both daylight and evening conditions.

In each of the five courts new centers of interest and spaces of rest were created with mosaic tile centered in new wood flooring. In keeping with local culture, tile patchwork quilt patterns were created to add a sense of environment. Each court features a different quilt design and the variety of patterns helps to create traffic flow between the courts. Garden style wood benches with latticework backs are set along the four sides of each quilt. Trees and plantings create an intimate space within the well-trafficked court.

The quilts are made of 12 in. squares of smaller tiles positioned as patches in the overall pattern, similar to real quilts. The squares were assembled at the factory facilitating the actual installation at the job site.

EXHIBIT DESIGN

"*E*xhibit design is the most complicated of design concepts. It has to excite, inform, influence and generate sales within a very short time frame. The designer must present the information in a format that is easily and quickly understood by the visitor.

The exhibit should be consistent with the marketing goals of the exhibitor, and convey a message that promotes the products and services presented.

Through the use of structure, color, graphics and lighting, the designer can produce an exhibit that greatly influences the visitor and further strengthens the goals of the clients."

LANDAU HEYMAN
ICSC CONVENTION
LAS VEGAS, NV

*L*andau Heyman, a Chicago-based developer, wished to create an exhibit that conveyed a fashion forward environment that would be conducive to conversation and property presentation.

To add visual strength to this small reception/display area, back illuminated photographs were used to identify the developers' properties. The walls were kept neutral to prevent interference with the light box images. The curved identification tower wrapped around the front reception desk encourages visitors to walk around the exhibit.

To create a sense of permanence, the seams of the modular curved wall panels were caulked after being erected at the show, and the walls were given a fresh coat of paint. Photos were prominently displayed, mounted on green tinted glass and back lighted by a concealed neon tube. The same green color used on the backwall was used in the upholstery.

The company logo curves around the identification tower and is rear-illuminated with neon tubing. The tower and walls are lit from above with 1000 watt spotlights. The counter was constructed from white oak and the frosted glass countertop was illuminated from below with neon.

MELVIN SIMON & ASSOCIATES
ICSC CONVENTION
LAS VEGAS, NV

*A*s one of the country's leading shopping center developers, Melvin Simon & Associates sought to create an environment that invited visitors to linger and learn about their business and properties.

Their booth was the largest exhibit at the ICSC convention, measuring 100 ft. by 110 ft. It was divided into reception areas, a showroom for presenting property information, dining, private offices and semi-private meeting rooms.

Identification was key for this developer, so four 24 ft. identification towers were constructed to add visibility on all four sides of this "island" exhibit. In addition to the four identification towers, back lighted graphics were mounted on the corners of all four sides of the exhibit to catch the attention of passing visitors.

The booth was divided into several smaller dining areas on all sides of the exhibit. Comfortable seating, planter boxes and umbrella tables helped to created the privacy needed to conduct meetings while dining. Around the 4,000 sq. ft. showroom located in the center of the exhibit were numerous semi-private meeting areas designed in an informal fash-ion. Numerous smaller private meeting rooms were located in the back of the exhibit for more private discussions.

The showroom in the center of the exhibit was designed as a gallery dedicated to the display of property information. Properties were rendered in an impressionistic style and illuminated with gallery lights. Rear projection screens were located in the center of the gallery promoting important properties.

*T*he LaSalle Partners of Chicago felt that it was important that the design of their exhibit space convey a message of financial strength, security, and a "sense of success in their ventures." To accomplish this, architectural elements were designed to add visual strength mixed with a sophisticated approach to retail.

The 24 ft. tall entrance tower was located on the corner of the busiest aisle, attracting visitors from four directions. Produced in faux finishes that represent stone, the tower made a striking presentation that could easily be seen throughout the convention center.

The company name was produced with 1/2 in. thick real brass and mounted on the face of a faux marble panel captured within the upper arch of the display. The pair of supporting columns, to either side of the opening, are also finished with faux green marble.

Identification signage made from brass cut letters is mounted to mahogany panels with brass inlay on each side of the booth. Illuminated light boxes present merchandise on two sides of the exhibit.

Side wall identification panels are finished with mahogany veneer with brass letters. The LaSalle Partners logo is cut from 1/2 in. solid brass and mounted on the mahogany panels at eye level.

A faux travertine floor with marble inlay marks the reception area.

MEPC
ICSC Convention
Las Vegas, NV

*T*his exhibit developed for European based MEPC was created in a circular design to encourage visitors to walk around the exhibit. Simple, but elegant in design details, this exhibit allows for maximum graphic presentation without confusion or over signing. A faux floor helped to further define the reception area. The receptionist located in the center of the space could easily greet all visitors approaching from three entrances.

To add visual strength to this small display area, rear illuminated transparency boxes and decorative light sconces were used. The walls remain neutral to avoid interfering with the light box images. The circular format of the display helps move traffic around the booth, preventing areas from becoming congested. The light sconces serve to define the graphic areas.

The circular reception desk sets the stage for the shape of the exhibit space. The circular display walls with transparency boxes sweep around the reception desk allowing the receptionist to greet visitors from any direction.

A post-modern entrance feature signs the booth, and designates the meeting room location. The MEPC logo is sharply defined with white letters in individual black squares.

The simple, sophisticated design of this exhibit and its graphic elements and furnishings enhances the strength and integrity of the developer and the properties displayed. The exhibit design should age well with time and repeated use.

PYRAMID
ICSC CONVENTION
LAS VEGAS, NV

*T*he Pyramid exhibit is a striking example of effective use of costly floor space. With exhibit space at a premium, this two-level exhibit was designed to fulfill a long list of exhibit requirements and provide a strong visual presence. Located on a corner, the exhibit is positioned to attract traffic from two directions. From this location the receptionist can greet all traffic from both aisles.

Food and drinks are served on the upper level, while in more private spaces on the lower floor, display and conference areas are arranged. The ceiling between the two floors controls the light levels over the showroom area, creating a dynamic environment for the presentation of property information.

Metal triangular pediments located atop the exhibit reflect the design of the company's logo and provide visibility from a distance. The exhibit was finished with off-white plastic laminate with black and red accents.

Staircases on
each side of the
exhibit lead to
the upper dining
level and add a
visual connec-
tive transition
between the two
levels.

To create a strong, fresh appearance that could be easily maintained for many years, a limited palette of colors and materials was used. All exhibit surfaces are finished with an off-white plastic laminate. Conference tables and furniture are finished with black plastic laminate with a gloss finish. Stackable chairs are used in the conference rooms while more expensive custom furnishings are in the display areas. Architecture and furnishings complement each other to produce an exhibit that will remain visually fresh for many years without expensive updates.

WESTFIELD
ICSC CONVENTION
LAS VEGAS, NV

*W*estfield is an Australian/USA-based developer with a strong presence in both markets. In fact, in Australia, a shopping center is referred to as a "Westfield." The design focus for this exhibit was to display the marketing strengths of this developer both nationally and internationally. To provide immediate visual impact, the booth was designed as a contemporary gallery focused on presenting property information in photographic form. The stark white walls and abundant spotlighting contrasts vividly with the strong colors and photo images.

Large identification overhead and at the booth front invites visitors into the space. Maintaining an open exposure allows visitors to freely walk in without a confrontation at the reception desk. Curved dimensional maps of Australia and the U.S. (halo lit with neon) sweep along a curved ten ft. high wall making a soft transition between the front reception area and the back meeting areas. Property photographs float off the wall between the two country maps creating a strong visual to attract visitors into the booth.

A curved identification sign mounted above vertical display photo towers provides strong visibility. The strong contrast of colors helps to emphasize the graphics.

Located in the back of the exhibit is a red architectural feature that serves to locate the entrance to the meeting rooms. The strong color and shape of the entrance helps create traffic flow to the back of the booth.

The "W" company logo mounted on a diagonal square reappears through-out the booth and a 36 ft. x 10 ft. photomural of Sydney, Australia mounted on the booth exterior announces the company's association with the Australian development market.

TRAMMELL CROW
ICSC CONVENTION
LAS VEGAS, NV

*T*o attract and bring shoppers into the Trammell Crow exhibit space, Horton used effective lighting and sharp color contrasts of warm and cool colors to achieve the desired effect. "In creating an environment, it is important to create contrasts of light and shadow when illuminating walls or display materials. By properly lighting an exhibit, you can control the traffic patterns."

To replicate the finishes from many of the client's properties, faux versions of these materials are used. To create a stone look, zolatone paints were applied to the walls. On the floors, plastic laminates are mounted on tempered masonite panels, and "V" grooves are cut into the laminate to indicate tile divisions.

The back curved wall of the exhibit space, behind the curve of the reception desk, is illuminated in a cool blue light sharply contrasting with the warm white "stone" finish of the surrounding architecture.

The property photographs and graphics are produced as color transparencies, back illuminated for brilliant color rendition. The brightness of the transparencies in contrast with the stone finishes of the display panels add strength to the graphics. A large cut-out map of the USA helps to impress visitors with Trammell Crow's national presence across the country.

In contrast to the cool blue and neutral wall colors, pink azaleas planted in terra cotta pots provide a softness to the space.

L J Hooker
ICSC Convention
Las Vegas, NV

*E*ntertainment is the focus for this large island exhibit. Brightly painted carousel horses mounted above the entrance and a circular reception desk, designed to suggest a colorful carousel, set the stage for this Las Vegas convention attraction.

Faux marble flooring, teal painted columns and ten ft. back-illuminated transparencies create the atmosphere for this 60 ft. wide reception area. Exaggerated vertical proportions help pull visitors into the space. To either side of the reception desk are comfortable seating areas for private conversation. Glass blocks, rear illuminated with blue neon, frame the back-lighted transparency panels, enhancing the graphics.

A painted metal pediment rests above the reception architecture creating visibility to the exhibit.

Easily visible just beyond the circular reception desk is pink neon signage announcing "George's Deli." The dining room was named for the chairman of the L J Hooker Group and was designed to be a fun, friendly and relaxed place for people to meet and eat. "It is exactly this kind of warm and inviting atmosphere that L J Hooker emphasized in the shopping centers developed by his firm."

The dining area is finished with marble patterned plastic laminates, black and white checkered floor tiles and lots of stainless steel accents to suggest a '50s style diner. Though mostly black and white, it sizzles with the pink glow over the space complemented by the cool blue vertical lighting fixtures.

HEITMAN PROPERTIES
ICSC CONVENTION
LAS VEGAS, NV

*I*nfluenced by the interior architectural details of the Heitman corporate offices in Chicago, Horton creates an environment that reflects the client's taste level and quickly conveys to the visitor the high caliber of the client's properties.

The design concept incorporates multiple finishes and colors both warm and cool, but close in value, to create a professional and inviting atmosphere. Back illuminated transparencies framed in hard rock maple veneer are recessed into bluish gray obelisks mounted between columns finished with maple veneer. A ten ft. signage tower located in the center of the space conceals the entrance into the meeting areas. A simple circular reception desk positioned in the center of the space coordinates with the frames around the graphic panels.

With a focus on the details and usage of quality materials, this exhibit projects an image of professionalism and sophistication. Modern wood veneer columns create warmth to offset the cool colors throughout the booth and add needed visual tension between the simplicity of the obelisks and the complexity of the curved capital details.

*F*or Homart, the Chicago-based developer, Horton creates a dramatic entrance into this exhibit. A procession of 12 ft. high columns focus attention to the client's logo positioned discreetly at the rear of the booth. Curved arches fabricated from metal angle and finished with a zolatone paint, cap each of the columns, creating an entrance feature that attracts visitors into the space.

Spaced between the columns are light box panels displaying important properties. The overhead light levels are reduced to create drama in the exhibit space allowing the back illuminated graphics to almost glow in the dim environment.

"To create an exhibit that would match the strengths and tastes of our client, we used all custom materials and furnishings. The displays were large enough in scale to provide the sense of being in a permanent environment."

Centrally-located graphics help to create an effective traffic flow for the exhibit. The back-lit photo transparencies are set into warm white walls and highlighted by raised gray frames. The frames are accented with teal keystones.

Furniture in charcoal gray and black with seating in small intimate groupings provide semi-private meeting areas. The faux finished floors add a reflective quality that strengthens the concept of permanence and also helps emphasize the scale of the exhibit components.

The simple geometry of the square furniture balances well with the vertical display components.

HERRING MARATHON
ICSC CONVENTION
LAS VEGAS, NV

*U*sing the glitter, glitz and total excitement that can be generated by an illuminated theater marquee, Tony Horton found a spectacular way to announce the opening of a new shopping center.

Over scaled identification letters, colorful neon lighting, display posters, and a rotating logo provide a unique sense of place to this exhibit. The ticket seller booth serves as the receptionist's desk in this novel setting.

The ceiling lights in the convention center seem to be an evening sky filled with a multitude of stars while the lights around the billboard periodically rotate to attract visitors. The neon bands on the underside of the marquee create a bright halo of light over the ticket booth. "This exaggerated illumination helps create a realistic movie night experience. Posters from the silver screen create nostalgia and add interest to the exhibit."

Inside, director chairs are used for seating and the canvas backs are printed with the names of properties developed by Herring Marathon.

EQUITY PROPERTIES
ICSC CONVENTION
LAS VEGAS, NV

*C*reating excitement was fundamental for this developer in their shopping centers and their convention exhibits. Believers in a strong visual marketing presentation, Equity Properties wanted an exhibit that conveyed the message that retail was about fun, excitement and entertainment.

What better way to get that message across than with balloons combined with bright colors, theatrical lighting and overscaled props.

"Bright colors, graphic patterns and lighting add impact to this small exhibit."

GLIMCHER
ICSC CONVENTION
LAS VEGAS, NV

*T*he design concept behind this exhibit for Glimcher is a circle within a circle. The inner circle contains the reception area and the outer circle displays the property graphics. The space between the two circles contains areas for seating and viewing the graphics.

The design objective was to create an exhibit that would "reflect the client's stature and reputation in the industry. The design had to represent style, strength and quality." These standards are achieved through the use of the dramatic architectural concepts and the execution of the design in real materials with special lighting and custom furniture.

To soften the physical scale of the exhibit, Horton specified a light palette of white blended with brushed aluminum and hard rock maple. The 24 ft. identification tower is finished with hard rock maple laminate. The logo is finished from brushed aluminum cut from 1/2 in. material. The walls are painted a pure white, on site, and the seams are caulked to give the modular wall panels the feel of one solid structure.

The floor is made in 4 ft. modular squares with #1 grade clear hard rock maple with inlays of brushed aluminum. The reception desk is finished with 1/4 in. curved brushed aluminum sheets. The counter is made from 1/2 in. tempered frosted glass, rear illuminated with white neon tubing. The central curved tower is painted, on site, a pure white, and illuminated with halogen lighting.

The 16 ft. circular tower is divided by the 24 ft. identification tower. The curved base finished with hard rock maple conceals a seating area.

Halogen light is reflected against curved frosted glass panels to provide ambient lighting around the perimeter of the exhibit.

ROCKWELL COLLINS
NBAA CONVENTION
LAS VEGAS, NV

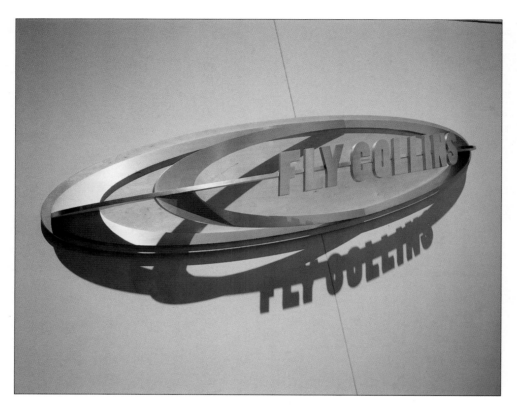

*R*ockwell Collins is one of the country's leaders in the innovation and production of communications equipment for the business aircraft industry. Tony Horton was challenged to create an exhibit that informed customers of both their history and continuing industry innovations.

"To keep the large volume of information understandable, we designed displays that clearly and simply identified specific information." The displays are positioned in a manner that promotes foot traffic through the exhibit. The displays are designed to deliver the information in a limited amount of time.

COLLINS SATCOM

MODEM THE REPORT TO NEW YORK,

MODEM THE REPORT TO NEW YORK,
CALL THE CLIENT IN LONDON,

CALL THE CLIENT IN LONDON,
FAX THE PHOTOS TO TOKYO,

FAX THE PHOTOS TO TOKYO,
ALL FROM 22,000 FEET—

ALL FROM 22,000 FEET—
ALL AT ONE TIME.

E TIME.

1993 - First Collins Satcom certified &
operating on a business jet.

To introduce new cockpit instrument controls, a unique sculpture that is representational of an aircraft nose cone was created. This proves an effective display technique and serves as a focal point in the exhibit layout. The sculpture is constructed from 3/4 in. Baltic birch "ribs." The design was detailed on a CAD program and machined on computer-aided shop equipment. Stainless steel hardware is used to connect the ribs.

On an adjacent wall, a cockpit instrument display is mounted on a birch panel and outlined with a cool neon light that makes the display float away from the back wall panel.

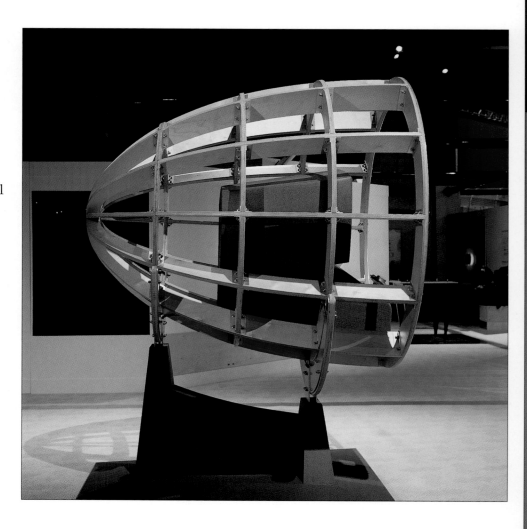

Elliptical-shaped grid screens float over each of the conference rooms. Their function is to reduce the convention lighting and glare to computer monitors and instrument displays. The screens are constructed from Baltic birch plywood and connected with stainless steel hardware.

Throughout, the designer uses design elements and building materials that reflect motion and the aviation industry.

In the dining area, Baltic birch fins are used to provide a degree of privacy for the individual dining tables. The design of these curved panels is inspired by the shape of aircraft. To limit shadows, the dividers are curved in the back to allow light to pass behind the panels.

The wall graphics between the fin dividers are raised away from the back wall and halo lit with neon tubing. The tables and chairs are finished with Baltic birch.

Curved aluminum ribs are used to display a new radio design.

EQUITY PROPERTIES
ICSC CONVENTION
LAS VEGAS

*T*o create a unique exhibit that reflects the marketing strengths of Equity, giant shopping bags were chosen to convey the message. The bags are fabricated from birch plywood panels finished with tempered masonite and painted with a lacquer finish. Strong colors create an impressive visual that is impossible to pass.

Ten ft. high shopping bags are positioned on each corner of the exhibit with company identification. Eight ft. high shopping bags fill the interior of the exhibit with 30 in. x 40 in. graphics mounted to each side. These panels provide property and company information.

Small, but still highly overscaled, shopping bags made from sheets of foam cover the display floor. These bags carry the Equity Properties logo to great heights above the convention floor and create a visual impact for the exhibit area while furthering the imagery of the shopping bag motif.

"Visual marketing presentation is as important on a convention floor as it is in a shopping center. It is important to create displays that excite but are not complicated, and inform but do not confuse. Simplicity is an accomplishment that is the most difficult to achieve," states Horton.

KIOSK DESIGN

*"T*he newest addition to retailing, in today's shopping centers, is the kiosk, or RMU (Retail Merchandising Unit).

Located in the common areas of most regional malls, the kiosk has to be limited in size, while providing substantial merchandising capabilities.

The visual strength of the kiosk plays an important part in the overall look of the shopping center, and the lighting, colors and materials used on the kiosks can greatly influence sales."

DISNEY
BEAUTY & THE BEAST

*I*n designing the Beauty & the Beast kiosks for the Disney Corporation, Tony Horton wanted the kiosks to feel animated. "To bring the kiosks to life, we created architectural elements that were very whimsical. The elements are very fluid with a sense of motion." These kiosks appear in Broadway theaters and serve as selling outposts for the show's merchandise.

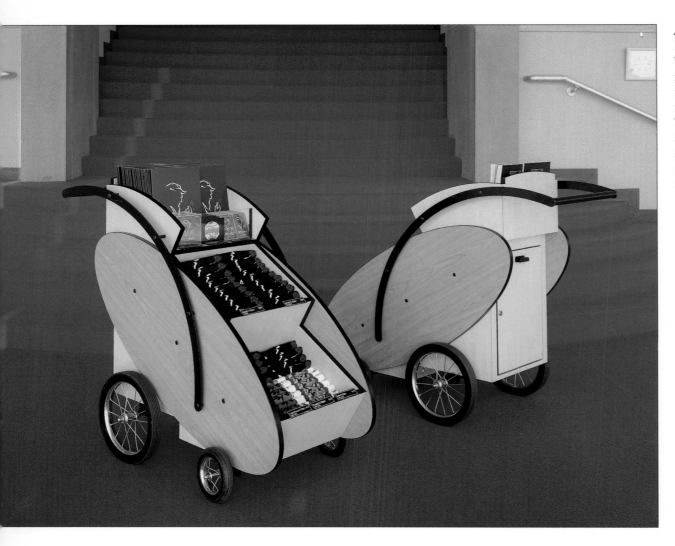

The kiosks were designed in three forms: kiosk, push cart, and a small merchandising carriage. The kiosk is used indoors. The push cart is used outdoors and stored indoors in the evenings. The small carriage can be pushed around to sell from any location during the show.

Horton selected pear and maple laminates with black accents to finish the kiosks. "We wanted rich colors that could stand on their own, but would not compete with the merchandise." Some kiosks are equipped with their own sources of lighting in the form of "goose" neck lamps that extend over the tops of light merchandise displayed below.

To provide ease of movement, the kiosks have large rubber casters. All the cases can be locked and the vertical displays are secured with roll down shutters.

EQUITY
PROPERTIES
CHICAGO, IL

*E*quity Properties is an innovator in the mall development industry and among the first to develop a kiosk program for its properties. Prior to the mid '80s, push carts, often with wagon wheels, were used in many malls as vehicles to promote the merchandise of temporary tenants. The push carts were often cumbersome and did not offer enough merchandising space to make the mobile unit profitable for the tenant. Equity contracted with Tony Horton to develop a merchandising display that focused on the presentation of merchandise and did not resemble a cart. The new creation was christened "RMU" (Retail Merchandising Unit) by Mark London, Sharon Palonia and Al Luthmers of Equity along with Tony Horton. The term and architectural style is now an industry standard.

"With the focus on successfully presenting merchandise, the wagon wheel was eliminated and lower level shelving was added. Fluorescent lights were replaced with low voltage halogen fixtures. Kiosks became taller and identification became more prominent. Support columns were slotted to allow for hanging merchandise."

YORK TOWN MALL
CHICAGO, IL

*T*he kiosks for the York Town Mall were designed by Tony Horton to "complement the architecture of the shopping center" and also to present a vast variety of merchandise.

The "Retail Merchandising Units" are built as 4 ft. x 4 ft. structures with wrap around shelving. To add additional visual weight to the design, Horton selected square columns with recessed slotted standards embedded in each side of the square posts. The columns are used to merchandise products and support the roof structure which is fabricated from copper sheet metal chemically treated to produce an antique, verdigris patina.

Each RMU is self-illuminated by internal and external light bars that replicate other metal work in the shopping center. The metal light bars are painted black and support low voltage tracks and light fixtures. The body of the kiosk is finished with a zolatone paint and accented with stone inlays.

*W*hen creating the RMUs or merchandising kiosks for specific mall use, Horton creates a design that blends with the center's architecture but is visually strong enough to stand out in the highly trafficked mall aisles. For Montgomery Mall, Horton created these 5 ft. x 5 ft. RMUs that are finished with cherry veneer accented with a warm white laminate and black powder coated metal.

The RMU was designed to be used with or without corner shelving. Merchandising corner displays were designed to replace the typical corner shelves to create a stronger display presentation. These corner displays ride on hidden casters and can be easily moved. The cash stand can be nested at any corner and can be incorporated into the RMU without taking away any of the valuable merchandising space.

The angled roof pediments recall the architecture in the center and the brass diamond insets relate to details on the center's soffits.

ANNAPOLIS MALL
ANNAPOLIS, MD

*T*o distinguish these RMUs in the corridors of the Annapolis Mall in Annapolis, Tony Horton added frosted plexiglass caps to the furniture-like fixtures that are finished with real cherry veneer. These panels are rear illuminated with glowing caps that create a strong visual, attracting shoppers. The curved shape of the plexiglass caps relates to the arched ceiling within the center.

Like the kiosks previously shown in the Bethesda, MD, center, these 5 ft. x 5 ft. RMUs have wrap around shelves that extend around the base. Corner displays can be added to increase the merchandising display space.

By using materials that are used in the mall finishes, these kiosks expand the overall retail environment while enhancing the shopping experience.

CLEVELAND INDIANS
CLEVELAND, OH

*T*he kiosks and carts designed by Horton for the Cleveland Indians baseball team are filled with nostalgic touches that recall "the good old days" of baseball. Designed to be used in and around the ballpark where crowds overwhelm, the space and visibility is a must for the RMU. These 3 ft. x 6 ft. kiosks are highlighted by pinstriped awnings, bright yellow tops and red metal cut-out flags. Ballpark fencing and wood siding are used to add to the ballpark concept.

The base of the kiosks are constructed of planks of wood painted a sharp white to provide a sense of nostalgia. The red color is used on the very bottom of the kiosk to edge the shelving. The red, blue and white Indians' logo appears on the wood base as well as on the yellow canvas top.

The kiosks are finished in neutral tones of gray and accented with black details.

*U*sed individually or clustered into "marketplaces," the RMUs, when designed to coordinate with the shopping center architecture, present the merchandise in an effective manner and add to the visual atmosphere of the mall interior. "Clustering kiosks is an effective method in creating a strong market environment. Customers can quickly and easily shop for many unique products in one location."

These 4 ft. x 4 ft. RMUs were designed with shelves that extend around the base, and can be substituted with glass cases or other merchandisers. The curved pediment and metal top is influenced by the center's architecture. Light bars with low voltage halogen fixtures extend over the shelving, providing strong lighting to the merchandise on all four sides of the kiosk. Square columns with recessed standards provide useful merchandising space for shelving or hanging merchandise.

TYSON GALLERIA
TYSON, VA

*C*reated to complement the center's architecture, these garden-like kiosks add visual strength to the products and increase the overall effectiveness of the court.

These kiosks are 3 ft. x 6 ft. and have shelving that wraps all four sides. The support columns are made from 4 in. steel tubing that is slotted to allow for merchandisers. The base and header are finished with a zola-tone paint. The pediment and brass details reflect the design of the center court.

As seen from this overhead view, the rectangular tops are supported by round columns with slotted holes for attaching merchandising brackets. The grid located in the header panel accommodates hanging displays, and provides security. Each kiosk is capped with a metal framework that recalls architectural details in the court.

Merchandising brackets attached to the round columns provide ample room for displaying hanging merchandise.

Designed to complement the sophistication of an upper scale market, these "urban"-style kiosks add quality and visual strength to any product. The kiosks' bases are finished in mahogany veneer with a deep mahogany stain. The header display is finished with a white satin painted finish. Sitting above the header are curved frosted glass panels finished in mahogany that serve as backdrops for tenant and center identification panels. The glass panels are rear illuminated to add a soft "glow" to the top. Recessed halogen fixtures in the header spotlight the product displays, and provide illumination around the kiosk.

GREAT MALL OF THE GREAT PLAINS
OLATHE, KS

Finished with plywood, exposed hardware, unfinished steel and aircraft cable, the kiosks for the Great Mall of the Great Plains work well in the industrial environment of the center.

*T*o work within the industrial environment of the Great Mall of the Great Plains, Tony Horton creates custom kiosks that redefine the term "industrial chic."

"To create a custom kiosk with an industrial look, construction grade materials had to be used. Based on the rawness of the materials, I didn't want to get too detailed with design. To work visually, industrial grade materials need to be treated simply, allowing the wonderful textures and patinas to create the character of the kiosk."

Baltic birch plywood is used on the base and shelves. Edges are left exposed on the shelving. The birch is finished with a top coat of clear polyurethane. Unfinished steel is used for the metal details. The metal is left in a semi-tarnished state, and finished with an invisible clear top coat to prevent the metal from further oxidizing. All connection hardware is left exposed and aircraft cable is stretched between the upper light bars.

FREMONT STREET EXPERIENCE
FREMONT STREET, LAS VEGAS, NV

The Fremont Street Experience is a dazzling, out in the open, free for all show of lights that has helped to turn downtown Las Vegas, the other resort/casino area, into a truly exciting tourist destination.

The "Experience" is built around a fabulous space frame that is 90 ft. high, spans a 125 ft. width and extends over 1400 linear feet. The management team asked Horton to design a kiosk that could display a wide array of products and withstand the extreme conditions created by the heat and sand. To withstand the extensive wear and tear of outdoor use, the kiosks were fabricated in metal finishes and painted with durable exterior paint. All hardware is stainless steel to prevent corrosive damage. Designed as a half circle, the shape works well with the large flow of traffic through the street. Riding on large casters, the kiosks can quickly be relocated for special events throughout the center.

To compete with the building signage and light show, the kiosks are taller than standard kiosks, reaching 12 ft. to the top of the "spears" that hold colorful banners. The overhanging canopy was fabricated from perforated metal, allowing visibility through the perforations. Halogen lights mounted below the perforated metal illuminate the lower level shelves and back light the canopy. A neon band around the top helps identify the kiosks.

SIERRA VISTA MALL
SIERRA VISTA, CA

*T*he kiosk was designed to display more product inventory than a typical kiosk, enhance visibility, and literally be a couple of feet shorter. "To accomplish these objectives I widened the lower merchandising area to 4 ft. x 8 ft. (6 ft. x 10 ft. with shelves) and staggered the base to allow better visibility and access to the products. By stair stepping the base I was able to increase lighting to the shelves and reduce the overall header size."

Although the kiosk appears smaller than a typical kiosk, it contains more merchandising space, is more merchantable, and is more easily shopped than a standard RMU.

Hard rock maple laminate is used to finish the body of the kiosk. All additional accents are black.

SUCCESSORIES
GARDEN STATE MALL, PARAMUS, NJ

To enhance the presentation of posters and printed materials, low voltage halogen lights are used to provide clear white lighting.

*"C*onsistency is key in developing product and name recognition." Successories realized that when they contracted with Tony Horton to design a kiosk, that would complement their store design.

To achieve immediate recognition in the mall aisle, a classic architectural pediment accented with a cherry cornice and cherry finished columns was designed to support the company identification. Other materials integrated into the design include a travertine marble laminate, a verdigris finished laminate and black and copper powder coated accents. The lower slatwall display fixtures are finished with verdigris laminate with a cherry trim.

WESTSIDE PAVILION
LOS ANGELES, CA

*T*he management of the recently renovated Westside Pavilion in Los Angeles called for a kiosk design that would "stand out in the crowd while complementing the architecture and materials found in the center."

The base of the RMU is finished in 16 gauge copper sheet metal that was chemically oxidized to create a verdigris finish. The column base corners are accented in metal that has been brightly finished with an automotive paint. Automotive and acrylic paints are used on the columns that support the curved roof and awnings. The arched top is capped at each end with copper sheet metal with a verdigris finish.

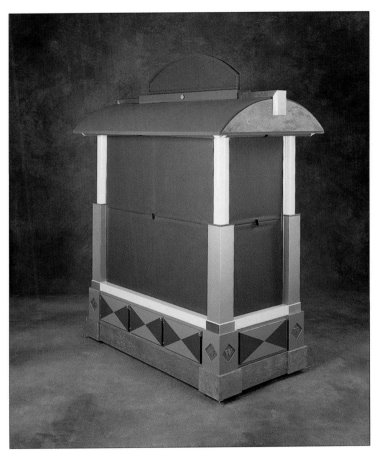

The particular requirement for this kiosk design was to withstand the ever-changing outdoor environment. To control the exterior exposure, all materials are weather resistant. The extended canvas awnings provide shade and prevent the sun and rain from damaging merchandise. When the kiosk is closed at night, the awnings fold down to secure the merchandise.

AWARDS

1999

1999 American Corporate Identity 2000
Award of Excellence
Trade Exhibit
Landau & Heyman, Chicago, IL

1998

American Corporate Identity 14
Award of Excellence
Signage/Environmental Graphic Design
Glimcher Realty Trust, Columbus, OH

American Corporate Identity 13
Award of Excellence
Signage/Environmental Graphic Design
West End Marketplace, Dallas, TX

American Corporate Identity 13
Award of Excellence
Signage/Environmental Graphic Design
Rockwell/Collins Avionics, Cedar
Rapids, IA

American Corporate Identity 13
Award of Excellence
Signage/Environmental Graphic Design
Zap at Stratosphere, Las Vegas, NV

Exhibitor
Design Excellence Awards Best Peninsula
Exhibit Design
Glimcher Realty Trust, Columbus, OH

1997

American Corporate Identity 12
Award of Excellence
Signage
Westfield, Inc., Los Angeles, CA

American Corporate Identity 11
Award of Excellence
Environmental Graphic Design
Southland Mall, Hayward, CA

American Corporate Identity 11
Award of Excellence
Environmental Graphic Design
Pavilion at the Old Post Office,
Washington, D.C.

American Corporate Identity 11
Award of Excellence Environmental
Graphic Design Union Station,
Indianapolis, IN

1996

The Institute of Store Planners
International Store Interior Design Awards
Honorable Mention
Environmental Graphic Design
West End Marketplace, Dallas, TX

Shopping Center World's
SADI Design Awards
Best Store 2000 sq. ft. - 5000 sq. ft., Best
New Specialty Store Design
BC Sports Collectable, Philadelphia, PA

*National Association of Store Fixture
Manufacturers*
Retail Design Competition
Grand Prize for Best Kiosk Design
Disney/Beauty and the Beast Retail,
Los Angeles, CA

*National Association of Store Fixture
Manufacturers*
Retail Design Competition
Merit Award, Best New Specialty Store
Design, Under 5000 sq. ft.
BC Sports Collectable, Philadelphia, PA

Graphic Design: USA
American graphic Design Award
Best Exhibit Design
MEPC, Dallas, TX

Graphic Design: USA
American graphic Design Award
Best Exhibit Design
Westfield, Inc., Los Angeles, CA

Graphic Design: USA
American graphic Design Award
Best Retail Project Design
West End Marketplace, Dallas, TX

1994

American Corporate Identity 9
Award of Excellence
Environmental Graphic Design
Southland Mall, Hayward, CA.

American Corporate Identity 9
Award of Excellence
Environmental Graphic Design
Union Station, Indianapolis, IN

American Corporate Identity 9
Award of Excellence
Environmental Graphic Design
The Pavilion at the Old Post Office,
Washington, D.C.

1991

Exhibitor
Design Excellence Award
Honorable Mention
Peninsula Exhibit Design
May Centers, Inc., St. Louis, MO

1990

Exhibitor
Design Excellence Awards
Honorable Mention
Peninsula Exhibit Design
Equity Properties & Development Co.,
Chicago, IL

International Council of Shopping Centers
MAXI Award
Best Exhibit Design
May Centers, Inc., St. Louis, MO

1989

Industrial Designers Society of America
Industrial Design Excellence Awards
Environmental Graphics Design
Southland Mall, CA Hayward, CA

Exhibitor
Design Excellence Awards
Best Double Deck Exhibit Design
The Pyramid Companies, Syracuse, NY

1988

Exhibitor
Design Excellence Awards
Best Peninsula Exhibit Design
Equity Properties and Development Co.,
Chicago, IL

1987

Communication Arts-87
Award of Excellence
Exhibit Design
Equity Properties and Development Co.,
Chicago, IL

1999

Kenyon, Kevin. (February 1999). Design consultant sees room for growth. *Shopping Centers Today*, 7-8.

Mattson, Beth. (February 1999). Coming of age. *Shopping Center World*, 63 68.

1998

(February 1998). Yorktown Shopping Center, Lombard, Illinois. *Shopping Center World*, cover.

Mayfield, Lisa. (February 1998). Design influences for specialty leasing programs. *Shopping Center World*, 44-52.

1996

(April 1996). Sade awards. Best store between 2000 & 5000 square feet. *Shopping Center World*, 32.

(November 1996). Batting a thousand. *VM+SD*, 46.

Faverman, Mark. (November 1996). The future of shopping center design. *Shopping Center World*, 19-23.

Hogan, Barbara A. (March 1996). Holiday temps add seasonal sparkle. *Shopping Centers Today*, 5-6.

1995

(February 1995). Coordinating the look. *Shopping Center World*.

1994

(May 1994). Successories sets own goals. *Shopping Center World*.

(May 1994). RMUs complement CenterMark mall. *Shopping Center World*.

Hogan, Barbara A. (February 1994). Customized carts can enhance a center. *Shopping Centers Today*, 14.

1993

(May 1993). Environmental graphics bring out center individuality. *Shopping Center World*, 143-146.

Hogan, Barbara A. (February 1993). Developers discovering gold. *Shopping Centers Today*, 1.

1991

Manson, Caryn B. (November 1991). Signage decisions can make or break image. *Shopping Center World*, 126-131.

1990

(May 1990). Color, decor changes revitalize Los Arcos. *Shopping Center World*, 330-336.

(September 1990). Maxi award play the winners, May Centers Inc., St. Louis. *Shopping Centers Today*, 73.

(September 1990). Union Station back on track. *Shopping Center World*, 38-39.

Baskin, Ellen. (December 1990). On the right track. *Designer's West*, 70-75.

McCloud, John. (November 1990). Malls respond to cry for increased service. *Shopping Center World*, 60-66.

Wallentine, Lois. (May 1990). Functional festivity. *Exhibitor*, 51.

1989

(May 1989). The winners. *Exhibitor*, May, 1989, 38-39.

DeFranks, Teresa. (May 1989). Designers talent spans trade mall, leasing mall and beyond. *Shopping Center World*, 4.

Mack, Robert E. (May 1989). Leasing mall: behind the scenes. *Shopping Centers Today*, 8-9.

Marlow, Paula. (May 1989). Pyramid presence. *Exhibitor*, 52-53.

1988

(May 1988). The winners. *Exhibitor*, 26-27.

(November 1988). TL Horton Design, Inc.: Southland Mall. *Designer's West*, 76.

Gade, Chris. (May 1988). "Bag warfare." *Exhibitor*, 36.

SELECTED BIBLIOGRAPHY
Published Projects in Books

1999

Carter, David E. (Ed.). (1996). Signage & environmental graphics, Landau & Heyman, Chicago, IL. *American Corporate Identity 2000* (p. 215). New York, NY: Hearst Books International.

1998

Carter, David E. (Ed.). (1996) Signage & environmental graphics, West End Marketplace, Dallas, TX. *American Corporate Identity/13* (p. 233). New York, NY: Hearst Books International.

Carter, David E. (Ed.). (1996). Signage & environmental graphics, Rockwell/Collins Avionics, Cedar Rapids, IA. *American Corporate Identity/13* (p. 234). New York, NY: Hearst Books International.

Carter, David E. (Ed.). (1996). Signage & environmental graphics, Zap at Stratosphere, Las Vegas, NV. *American Corporate Identity/13* (p. 237). New York, NY: Hearst Books International.

1997

Carter, David E. (Ed.). (1996). Signage & environmental graphics, Faison Associates, Charlotte, NC. *American Corporate Identity/12* (p. 205). New York, NY: Art Direction Book Co.

Carter, David E. (Ed.). (1996). Signage & environmental graphics, Westfield, Inc., Los Angeles, CA. *American Corporate Identity/11* (p. 209). New York, NY: Art Direction Book Co.

1996

Carter, David E. (Ed.). (1996). Signage & environmental graphics, Union Station, Indianapolis, IN. *American Corporate Identity/11* (p. 214). New York, NY: Art Direction Book Co.

Carter, David E. (Ed.). (1996). Signage & environmental graphics, Southland Mall - Equity Properties & Development, Hayward, CA. *American Corporate Identity/11* (p. 21 5). New York, NY: Art Direction Book Co.

Carter, David E. (Ed.). (1996). Signage & environmental graphics, Pavilion at the Old Post Office, Washington, DC. *American Corporate Identity/11* (p.21 6). New York, NY: Art Direction Book Co.

1995

Pegler, Martin M. (Ed.). (1995). Home, fashions, entertainment, Successories, Prudential Center, Boston, Massachusetts. *Stores of the Year/9* (pp. 194-195). New York, NY: Retail Reporting Corporation.

Carter, David E . (Ed .). (1995). Signage & environmental graphics, Los Arcos Mall, Scottsdale, AZ. *American Corporate Identity/10* (p. 180). New York, NY: Art Direction Book Co.

Carter, David E. (Ed.). (1995). Signage & environmental graphics, York Galleria, York, PA. *American Corporate Identity/10* (p. 183). New York, NY: Art Direction Book Co.

Carter, David E. (Ed.). (1995). Signage & environmental graphics, Regency Square, Florence, AL. *American Corporate Identity/10* (p. 184). New York, NY: Art Direction Book Co.

Carter, David E. (Ed.). (1995). Signage & environmental graphics, Southgate Plaza, Sarasota, FL. *American Corporate Identity/10* (p. 187). New York, NY: Art Direction Book Co.

Salb, Joan G. (Ed.). (1995). Omnium - Gatherum: A surprising diversity of retailers, Successories, Celex Group, Inc., Lombard, IL. *Retail Image and Graphic Identity* (p.190-191). New York, NY: Retail Reporting Corporation.

1994

Konikow, Robert B. (1994). The giants on the floor, Homart Development Co. *Exhibit Design 6* (pp.90-91). Glen Cove,NY: PBC international, Inc.

Konikow, Robert B. (1994). The giants on the floor, MayCenters/Centermark Properties. *Exhibit Design 6* (pp. 114 - 117). Glen Cove, NY: PBC International, Inc.

1992

Kaye, Gordon (Ed.). (1992). Retail/shopping centers, Union Station. *Environmental Graphics, Sign Design* (pp. 92-95). Glen Cove, NY: PBC International, Inc.

Kaye, Gordon (Ed.). (1992). Retail/shopping centers, Southland Mall Food Court, *Environmental Graphics, Sign Design* (pp. 98-99). Glen Cove, NY: PBC International, Inc.

Kaye, Gordon (Ed.). (1992). Retail/shopping centers, Los Arcos Mall, Southgate Plaza, *Environmental Graphics, Sign Design* (p. 106). Glen Cove, NY: PBC International, Inc.

Kaye, Gordon (Ed.). (1992) Retail/shopping centers, Southgate Plaza, *Environmental Graphics, Sign Design* (p.107). Glen Cove, NY: PBC International, Inc.

Kaye, Gordon (Ed.). (1992) Retail/shopping centers, Fox River Mall, *Environmental Graphics, Sign Design* (p.107). Glen Cove, NY: PBC International, Inc.

Barr, Vilma. (1992). signs, Union Station. *The Best of Neon* (p. 184). Rockport, MA: Rockport Publishers, Inc.

1991

Industrial Designers Society of America (Ed.). (1991). Environmental design, bronze award for Equity Properties and Development Co., Southland Mall. *Designing For Humanity* (pp. 150-151). Glen Cove, NY: PBC International, Inc.

Pegler, Martin M. (Ed.). (1991). Food courts, Union Station Food Court. *Food Presentation & Display* (pp.214-215). New York, NY: Retail Reporting Corporation.

Phillips, Alan (Ed.). (1991). Office design, modern, TL Horton Design, Inc. *The Best in Office Interior Design* (pp. 88-90). Mies, Switzerland: Rotovision SA.

1988

Konikow, Robert B. (Ed.). (1988). Medium exhibits, Donohoe O'Brien. *Exhibit Design 3* (p. 72). Glen Cove, NY: PBC International, Inc.

Konikow, Robert B. (Ed.). (1988). Large exhibits, Equity Properties and Development Co. *Exhibit Design 3* (p. 92). Glen Cove, NY: PBC International, Inc.

Konikow, Robert B. (Ed.). (1988). Large exhibits, Goodman Segar Hogen. *Exhibit Design 3* (p. 93). Glen Cove, NY: PBC International, Inc.

Konikow, Robert B. (Ed). (1988). Giant exhibits, Homart Development Co. *Exhibit Design 3* (pp. 114-115). Glen Cove, NY: PBC International, Inc.

Konikow, Robert B. (Ed.). (1988). Giant exhibits, Melvin Simon & Associates. *Exhibit Design 3* (pp. 117-119). Glen Cove, NY: PBC International, Inc.

Konikow, Robert B. (Ed.). (1988). Giant exhibits, Herring Marathon Group. *Exhibit Design 3* (p.120). Glen Cove, NY: PBC International, Inc.

Konikow, Robert B. (Ed.). (1988). Showrooms and offices, TL Horton Design, Inc. *Exhibit Design 3* (pp. 200-201). Glen Cove, NY: PBC International, Inc.

TONY HORTON SELECTED PROJECT LIST

1999

Exhibits

Jones Lang LaSalle
Atlanta, GA

Rockwell Collins Avionics
Cedar Rapids, IA

Office

Tony Horton, Inc.
24,000 Sq. Ft. Office/studio
2824 Canton Street, Dallas, TX

1998

Exhibit

Trus Joist MacMillian
Boise, ID

1997

Exhibits

Rockwell Collins Avionics
Cedar Rapids, IA

Trus Joist MacMillian
Boise, ID

1996

Retail Store Design

Java City, Suburban Station
Philadelphia, PA

Java City, Liberty Mall
Philadelphia, PA

Zap
Grapevine Mills Mall
Dallas, TX

Retail Merchandise Displays

Walt Disney Company
The Lion King
New Amsterdam Theatre
New York, NY

1995

Retail Store Design

Celex Group/ Successories
(28) US Malls

Zap
The Stratosphere
Las Vegas, NV

Retail Merchandise Displays

Walt Disney Company
Beauty & The Beast
The Palace Theatre
New York, NY

Walt Disney Company
Beauty & the Beast
Orpheum Theatre
Chicago, IL

Walt Disney Company
Beauty & The Beast
US National Road Tour

Walt Disney Company
Beauty & The Beast
Canada, Europe, Japan

Fremont Street Experience
Las Vegas, NV

Exhibits

Faison
Charlotte, NC

The Glimcher Companies
Columbus, OH

Insignia
Houston, TX

MEPC
Dallas, TX

Rockwell Collins Avionics
Cedar Rapids, IA

Saul Company
Bethesda, MD

Turnberry & Associates
Turnberry, FL

Westfield, Inc.
Los Angeles, CA

1994

Retail Store Design

B C Sports Collectables
Bear, PA

Celex Group/Successories
(25) US Malls

Zap
Sawgrass Mills Mall
Sawgrass, FL

Retail Merchandise Displays

Walt Disney Company
Beauty & The Beast
Schubert Theatre
Los Angeles, CA

Exhibits

Gibraltar
Tarrytown, NY

The O'Connor Group
New York, NY

**Architectural Re-Design &
Environmental Graphics**

The West End Marketplace
Dallas, TX

1993

Retail Store Design

Celex Group/Successories
(3) US Malls

Exhibits

Enterprise Development Company
Baltimore, MD

Federal Realty, Inc.
Bethesda, MD

Kravco
Philadelphia, PA

Marathon
Dallas, TX

National Realty, Inc.
Purchase, NY

Rockwell Collins Avionics
Cedar Rapids, IA

Environmental Graphics

North Pier Shopping Center
Chicago, IL

York Galleria
York, PA

1992

Exhibits

Centermark Properties
St. Louis, MO

Combined Properties
Washington, DC

Maremagnum
Barcelona, Spain

Rubloff
Chicago, IL

Environmental Graphics

Fox River Mall
Fox River, WI

The Pavilion at The Old Post Office
Washington, D.C.
.

Retail Merchandise Displays

Green Acres Mall
Valley Stream, NY

Swire Properties
Hong Kong

1991

**Architectural Re-Design
Environmental Graphics**

The Falls Shopping Center
Miami, FL

Richland Mall
Johnstown, PA

Exhibits

Heitman Retail Properties
Chicago, IL

1990

Exhibits

Combined Properties
Washington, DC

Enterprise Development Company
Baltimore, MD

Homart Development Company
Chicago, IL

May Centers, Inc.
St. Louis, MO

The Shopco Group
New York, NY

**Architectural Re-Design
Environmental Graphics**

Magnolia Mall
Florence, AL

Union Station
Indianapolis, IN

Environmental Graphics
The Century Shopping Center
Chicago, IL

1989

Exhibits

Donohoe O'Brien
Philadelphia, PA

Equity Properties and Development
Company
Chicago, IL

The Glimcher Companies
Columbus, OH

La Salle Partners
Chicago, IL

The Pyramid Companies
Syracuse, NY

Shopping Centers Today
New York, NY

Shopping Center World
Atlanta, GA

Volume Shoe
Topeka, KA

**Architectural Re-Design
Environmental Graphics**

Los Arcos Mall
Scottsdale, AZ

Swansea Mall
Swansea, MA

Environmental Graphics

Southgate Mall
Sarasota, FL

Turfland Mall
Lexington, KY

1988

Exhibits

BCED
Chicago, IL

B.F. Saul Company
Bethesda, MD

Burger King
Miami, FL

Rockwell Collins Avionics
Cedar Rapids, IA

Continental Development
Company
Meridian, MS

Edward Plant Company
San Francisco, CA

Goodman Segar Hogan
Norfolk, VA

Homart Development Company
Chicago, IL

Joseph Freed and Associates
Chicago, IL

Landgrant Development
San Diego, CA

La Salle Partners
Chicago, IL

The Lehndorff Company
Dallas, TX

L. J. Hooker Development
Atlanta, GA

MacMillan Blodel
Boise, ID

Rreef
San Francisco, CA

Richard I. Rubin
Philadelphia, PA

The Sizeler Company
New Orleans, LA

Trammell Crow Company
Dallas, TX

Washington Area Developers
Washington, DC

Westfield, Inc.
Los Angeles, CA

Zaremba
Cleveland, OH

Environmental Graphics
Mall at 163rd Street
Miami, FL

**Architectural Re-Design
Environmental Graphics**
Southland Mall
Hayward, CA

1987

Exhibits

Donohoe O'Brian
Philadelphia, PA

Federal Realty, Inc.
Bethesda, MD

Homart Development Company
Chicago, IL

1986

Exhibits
Dimension Development
Companies
Dallas, TX

Equity Properties and Development
Company
Chicago, I L

Herring Marathon
Dallas, TX

Melvin Simon and Associates
Indianapolis, IN

The O'Connor Group
New York, NY

Paul Broadhead & Associates
Meridian, MS

1985

Exhibits

Arthur M. Fischer
St. Louis, MO

Crown American
Johnstown, PA

The Herring Group
Dallas, TX

Kravco
Philadelphia, PA

Melvin Simon & Associates
Indianapolis, IN

Payless Shoesource
Topeka, KA

**In addition to the Selected Project
List, Tony Horton has designed
Retail Merchandising Displays for
over 500 shopping malls worldwide.
A partial list of developers includes;**

Cadillac Fairview Corp., Ltd.

Copaken White & Blitt

Corporate Property Investors

Crown American Properties

Debartolo Company

Equity Properties and Development
Company

Faison & Associates

Forest City Development

General Growth Properties

The Glimcher Companies

Harlem Irving Plaza

Heitman Retail Properties

Homart Development Company

The Irvine Company

The Jacobs Group

Jones Lang La Salle

JP Realty

Kravco

Macerich Company

Plaza Associates

Preit Rubin, Inc.

Pyramid Companies

Turnberry Associates

Urban Retail Properties

Wellspark Group

Westfield, Inc.

Zions Securities

ACKNOWLEDGEMENTS

*T*his book is dedicated to Kim Webb, my wife and business partner, for her support, her love and her continuing dedication to my work. Without her, my work and this book would only be a dream.

This book is also dedicated to my children, Blake, Bryce and Anna Beth for supporting me when I had to miss those special moments in their lives. Their love was always with me, and mine with them.

And, this book is dedicated to the many clients who allowed me to seek my own direction in creating their projects, and to the many clients that pushed me to achieve my very best.

I would like to give a special thanks to several people that have been instrumental in many ways during my career. Dutch Antonisse and Gene Rogowicz for giving a poor art student a chance. Mark London for understanding and promoting the vision. Al Luthmers for teaching me how to observe the obvious. Cheri Morris and Ann Taradash for their experience and creative direction. Gene Schwarting and Diana Fairchild for believing in me and allowing me to do my best work.

I have learned a great deal from the five hundred plus people that have so tirelessly worked for me over the last seventeen years. Words cannot express my gratitude for their support, dedication and talents.

*T*he efforts of the following staff members have played a significant role in our success. Thank you for all the years of dedication, hard work and loyalty. I will never forget your contributions.

Don Arient
Don Barker
Krystyna Bojanowski
Clayton Broders
John Buhler
Steve Byford
Ken Clasen
Jim Connor
Mike Cullen
Dan Dorn
Stanley Gilbert
John Goforth
Alvino Gonzales
Jerald Green
Yvonne Hahn
Gus Hamsho
Houston Hartley
Julian Hernandez
Andrew James
Robert Johnson
Paul Johnston
Shannon Juett
Matt Kaser
Emmett Keown
Wayne Keown
Bruce Kirby
David Martin

Paul May
Rob McCoy
John Messmer
Dean Moss
Don Neveling
Alan Ouellet
Nanette Palomo
Marsha Pyron
Roy Raines
Rita Randolph
John Reger
Earl Robertson
David Shaulis
Bobby Simons
Karla Soliz
Henry Smith
Tim Smith
Manuel Solis
Jerald Thompson
Wayne Tutt
Eric Valenzuela
Mike VanPamel
Donna Wawak
Jerianne Welsh
Bill Wilkins
Damon Wilkins
Karen Willis

One of the greatest joys of my career has been the opportunity to work with some of the very best photographers in the business. Their vision and talents have worked together to create truly remarkable photo images.

Although I have used several others, Joe Aker and his partner Gary Zvonkovic of Aker/Zvonkovic Photography have photographed the majority of the projects in this book. Joe and Gary's talents and skills, apparent in this volume, have contributed greatly to the successful presentation of these projects. Their extensive skills, expertise and diligence have always made them the right choice for any assignment.

All photos except as noted
Joe Aker
Gary Zvonkovic
Aker/Zvonkovic Photography
4710 Lillian Street
Houston, Texas 77007
713.862.6343

The Pavilion (Cover)
Barth Tillotson
Tillotson Photography
2511 Swiss Avenue
Dallas, Texas 75204
214.352.9590

Java City
Tom Bernard Photography
586 Conestoga Road
Berwyn, Pennsylvania 19312
610.296.9289

Great Mall of the Great Plains
Forwell Studio
210 N. Glenwood Avenue
Dalton, Georgia 30721
706.226.2208

INDEX BY PROJECTS

Annapolis Mall, Annapolis, MD, *150*
B C Sports Collectables, Bear, PA, *14*
Cleveland Indians, Cleveland, OH, *152*
Copley Place, Boston, MA, *160*
Disney, Beauty & the Beast, *140*
Enterprise, ICSC Convention, Las Vegas, NV *118*
Equity Properties, Chicago, IL, *144*
Equity Properties, ICSC Convention, Las Vegas, NV, *114*
Equity Properties, ICSC Convention, Las Vegas, NV, *134*
Fairfield Commons, Fairfield, OH, *154*
Fremont Street Experience, Fremont Street, Las Vegas, NV, *164*
Glimcher, ICSC Convention, Las Vegas, NV, *120*
Great Mall of The Great Plains, Olathe, KS, *162*
Heitman Properties, ICSC Convention, Las Vegas, NV, *102*
Herring Marathon, ICSC Convention, Las Vegas, NV, *110*
Homart, ICSC Convention, Las Vegas, NV, *106*
Java City, Philadelphia, PA, *24*
L J Hooker, ICSC Convention, Las Vegas, NV, *98*
Landau Heyman, ICSC Convention, Las Vegas, NV, *74*
LaSalle Partners, ICSC Convention, Las Vegas, NV, *80*
Melvin Simon & Associates, ICSC Convention, Las Vegas, NV, *76*
MEPC, ICSC Convention, Las Vegas, NV, *82*
Montgomery Mall, Bethesda, MD, *148*
Pyramid, ICSC Convention, Las Vegas, NV, *86*
Regency Square, Florence, AL, *68*
Rockwell Collins, NBAA Convention, Las Vegas, NV, *126*
Sierra Vista Mall, Sierra Vista, CA, *167*
Southgate, Sarasota, FL, *60*
Southland Mall, Hayward, CA, *54*
Successories, Garden State Mall, Paramus, NJ, *168*
Successories, Prudential Center, Boston, MA, *26*
T L Horton Design, Inc. Offices, Dallas, TX, *8*
The Pavilion, Washington, DC, *50*
Trammell Crow, ICSC Convention, Las Vegas, NV, *94*
Tyson Galleria, Tyson, VA, *156*
Union Station, Indianapolis, IN, *34*
West End Marketplace, Dallas, TX, *62*
Westfield, ICSC Convention, Las Vegas, NV, *90*
Westside Pavilion, Los Angeles, CA, *170*
York Galleria, York, PA, *42*
York Town Mall, Chicago, IL, *146*
ZAP, Stratosphere Hotel/Casino, Las Vegas, NV, *20*